Living in the Raw

Desserts

Rose Lee Calabro

Book Publishing Company
Summertown, Tennessee

Cover design: Warren Jefferson
Photography: Warren Jefferson
Food styling: Barbara Jefferson, Melina Bloomfield
Interior design: Gwynelle Dismukes

Published in the United States by
Book Publishing Company
P.O. Box 99
Summertown, TN 38483
1-888-260-8458
www.bookpubco.com

Printed in Canada

ISBN 978-1-57067-201-9

12 11 10 09 08 07   6 5 4 3 2 1

The contents of this book are a reflection of the author's experience and are in no way intended to take the place of professional medical treatment. The author does not dispense medical advice nor prescribe the use of any technique as a form of treatment for physical, mental, or emotional health challenges, with or without the advice of a physician.

To contact Rose Lee Calabro: phone 877-557-4711
e-mail: livingintheraw1@hotmail.com

Calabro, Rose Lee.
  Living in the raw desserts / Rose Lee Calabro.
     p. cm.
  Includes index.
  ISBN 978-1-57067-201-9
  1. Desserts. 2. Raw foods. I. Title.

TX773.C244 2007
641.8'6--dc22
                    2006039304

The Book Publishing Co. is a member of Green Press Initiative. We have elected to print this title on paper with 10% postconsumer recycled content and processed chlorine free, which saved the following natural resources:

5 trees
115 lbs of solid waste
11 lbs of greenhouse gases
1 million BTUs

BOOK
PUBLISHING
COMPANY

For more information visit: www.greenpressinitiative.org. Savings calculations thanks to the Environmental Defense Paper Calculator at www.papercalculator.org

With God's blessings, guidance, and inspiration
this book was created.

Dedication

To my children, I love you.
Keith M. Adams
Kerrie L. Adams, M.D.

Also, I dedicate this book to you, the reader, for being interested enough to purchase it. I hope you find it fun and creative to discover a new way of creating healthful desserts. This book was created with much love in the hope that everyone will enjoy creating raw food dishes.

Special thanks to:

A. Annette Hulett, *M.A., for her love, guidance, and support on my healing path;*

Nicol Sanks, *for her friendship, love, and support on my healing path;*

Virginia Shaeffer, *for her friendship, love, and support on my healing path;*

Michelle Van de Voorde, *for contributing ingredients, allowing me to use her kitchen to test the recipes, and giving me feedback.*

Contents

Introduction

The raw desserts in this book are simple to prepare, healthful, outrageously delicious, and spectacular to serve. The recipes have simple and clear instructions; so, if you have never made raw desserts before, you will be amazed how easy they are to prepare and how incredibly delicious they are. They are perfect for special occasions, and your guests will be grateful for a dessert that is nutritious. No wheat, sugar, eggs, or unhealthful additives are included in any of the recipes. All of the ingredients used in this book are raw and available from a natural food store.

Cakes are the highlight of many celebrations. What birthday would be complete without a cake with candles to blow out? What wedding would be complete without a beautiful cake to cut? Recipes can be found in this book to create the most outrageous raw cakes in the world.

Raw dessert recipes can range from the lightest mousse to the most decadent carob cake, so there are several decisions to be made when planning a menu. Your choice of what to serve will be influenced by the season and the occasion. If you are serving a filling main course, you will invariably choose a light or fruity dessert to follow it; if you plan to make a rich, creamy dessert, you will deliberately pick a light main course. To help you maintain a healthful balance, this book includes a wide range of delicious desserts that can make the decision reassuringly easy.

Many of the desserts in this book can be made a day or two in advance; others can be started early in the day and finished just before you eat; and frozen desserts and ice creams can be made several days in advance, ready to serve whenever you need them. If you are planning a festive meal or entertaining a large number of people, make sure you leave plenty of time for preparation. Choose one of the desserts that can be made in advance, and do at least some of the work for the other courses earlier in the day. That way your guests and you can enjoy the meal.

Equipment

There are four basic pieces of equipment you will need to create the raw desserts in this book:

- Blender, heavy duty (I recommend the Vita-Mix or BlendTec Total Blender)
- Dehydrator (I recommend the Excalibur Dehydrator), with Teflex sheets
- Food Processor (I recommend a Cuisinart food processor)
- Juicer, electric (I prefer the Champion Juicer)

Why Organic?

Organic: Food produced without the use of chemically formulated fertilizers, growth stimulants, antibiotics, or pesticides.

All food is not created equal. The nutrition content of organically grown produce is superior. It is higher in vitamins, minerals, and naturally occurring enzymes, which make the nutrients in organic food more easily digested and absorbed. Organic food is not only more healthful, the flavor is incredibly delicious.

Organic food is better for us as consumers and for the planet, which directly affects our health as well. Unfortunately, chemical inputs cause extensive damage to our environment; but the inverse is equally astounding. Organic growing methods decrease pesticide contamination, enrich the soil, protect wildlife, safeguard water resources, are economically sound and health supporting, and encourage a self-sustaining ecosystem.

Buy fresh and organic ingredients! The desserts will taste only as good as the ingredients that go into them. It is extremely important to buy fresh and organic produce, preferably from a farmers' market where the produce is picked that morning or the night before it is sold.

Always choose organic food—it's the right choice for you and the planet!

Young Coconuts

Coconuts are one of the most healthful foods we can eat. Coconuts are rich in lauric acid, a fatty acid with antibacterial, antiviral, antifungal, and anti-inflammatory properties. Coconut water is nearly identical to human blood plasma and is known to have been used in emergency transfusions. Coconut water is high in potassium, copper, iron, calcium, ascorbic acid (vitamin C), and the B-complex vitamins.

Aside from the health benefits, the young coconut's pulp and water are simply delightful and delicious and have been used in many of the recipes in this book. They are available at Asian markets and some natural food stores. I recommend buying them by the case so you will always have some on hand. Coconuts will last one to three weeks when stored in the refrigerator. Locating young coconuts in your area is definitely worth the effort. They are extremely healthful and make fabulous desserts.

Soaking Nuts and Seeds

Raw nuts and seeds are an essential staple of the raw living food diet. It is extremely important to always purchase RAW, unroasted nuts and seeds to prepare the recipes in this book. Roasted nuts and seeds are not capable of sprouting, because the heat used in the roasting process destroys their ability to germinate. Raw nuts and seeds that are soaked and sprouted become more nutritious and are rich in enzymes.

Soaking should be done in any nonmetallic container. I like to use glass jars. Nuts and seeds should be soaked in purified water, then drained and rinsed every eight hours. Fresh water may be added, or simply proceed as directed in the recipe.

Once nuts or seeds are removed from their protective shells, there is the possibility that the essential oils they contain can become rancid. To prevent this,

Introduction

store raw nuts and seeds in a sealed, airtight glass container in a cool, dry location. Also, you can keep them in the refrigerator for up to a month and in the freezer for up to six months.

Blanching Almonds

Blanching removes the brown skin of shelled almonds. It's easy and quick to do, and blanching enhances the color and flavor of many dishes. Soak the almonds for 12–48 hours (I prefer to soak mine for 48 hours). Soaked almonds are richer in enzymes, and their skins are a lot easier to remove. Drain and transfer them to a heatproof bowl. Pour boiling water over the almonds to cover them completely. Let them rest for 30–60 seconds, just until the skins are loosened. Drain the boiling water and add some warm water. This helps to keep the almonds moist and will facilitate the removal of the skin. Peel the almonds by squeezing them between your index or middle finger and thumb. The skins should slide off easily.

Remember that all the nuts and seeds used in this book are raw, not roasted!

Cakes

If your food processor is small, you might have difficulty processing a full cake recipe in it. In that case, simply process one-half or one-third of the recipe at a time; then combine the portions in a bowl to finish the recipe.

Many of my cake recipes call for dates. I prefer medjool dates or honey dates for making cakes, as they are moist, meaty, and soft. Also, the dates will blend better with the nuts if they are at room temperature.

German Mock Chocolate Cake

Yield: 8–10 servings

Cake

2 cups	almonds, soaked 12–48 hours
2 cups	pitted medjool dates
6 tablespoons	raw carob powder
2 teaspoons	vanilla extract

Place the almonds in a food processor fitted with the S blade, and process into a fine meal. Gradually add the dates, carob powder, and vanilla extract, and process until the mixture forms a small ball. Transfer to a cake plate or round serving platter, and form into a 10-inch round cake.

Icing

1 cup	young coconut pulp
1/2 cup	pecans, soaked 1 hour
1 teaspoon	vanilla extract

Combine all the ingredients in a blender, and process until smooth and creamy. Add a small amount of water, if needed, to achieve the desired consistency. The icing should be thick, smooth, and creamy. Spread the icing evenly on top of the cake.

Topping

½ cup	unsweetened shredded dried coconut
¼ cup	walnuts, chopped

Sprinkle the coconut and walnuts evenly on top of the icing. Refrigerate for 2–3 hours before serving.

Cakes

Carrot Cake

Yield: 10–12 servings

This cake can only be made in a Champion Juicer or a Green Power Juicer.

Cake

3 cups	chopped carrots
1 cup	almonds, soaked 12–48 hours and blanched (see page 10)
1/2 cup	pitted medjool dates
1/4 cup	pine nuts, soaked 1 hour
1	apple, cored
1/2 cup	raisins
1/2 cup	walnuts, soaked 1 hour and chopped
1/4 cup	unsweetened shredded dried coconut
1 tablespoon	psyllium powder
1 teaspoon	vanilla extract
1/2 teaspoon	ground cinnamon
1/2 teaspoon	ground cardamom
1/2 teaspoon	Celtic salt
1/4 teaspoon	ground nutmeg

Process the carrots, almonds, dates, pine nuts, and apple through a Champion Juicer fitted with the solid plate. Transfer to a bowl, and stir in the remaining ingredients. Mix well. Press firmly into an 8 x 8-inch glass dish.

Icing

¾ cup	macadamia nuts, soaked 2 hours
¼ cup	pitted medjool dates
¼ cup	pine nuts, soaked 1 hour
¼ cup	water
2 tablespoons	fresh lemon juice
2 teaspoons	vanilla extract

Combine all the ingredients in a blender, and process until smooth, thick, and creamy. Spread the icing over the cake. Refrigerate for 1–2 hours before serving.

Cakes

Strawberry Torte

Torte

2 cups	almonds, soaked 12–48 hours
2 cups	pitted medjool dates
2 teaspoons	vanilla extract

Place the almonds in a food processor fitted with the S blade, and process into a fine meal. Gradually add the dates and vanilla extract, and process until the mixture forms a small ball. Transfer to a cake plate or round serving platter, and form into an 8-inch round torte.

Icing

1 cup	macadamia nuts or cashews, soaked 1 hour
1 cup	strawberries, stems removed
1/4 cup	pitted dates, soaked 1 hour
1 teaspoon	vanilla extract

Combine all the ingredients in a blender, and process until smooth, thick, and creamy. Spread the icing over the torte.

Topping

     2 cups   sliced strawberries, stems removed

Arrange the strawberries decoratively on top of the icing.

Decoration for the Sides

     ½ cup   hazelnuts, finely chopped

Press the chopped hazelnuts into the sides of the torte. Refrigerate the torte for 2–3 hours before serving.

Hazelnut Carob Torte

Yield: 8–10 servings

Torte

2 cups	hazelnuts, soaked 1 hour
2 cups	pitted medjool dates
4 tablespoons	raw carob powder
1 teaspoon	vanilla extract

Place the hazelnuts in a food processor fitted with the S blade, and process into a fine meal. Gradually add the dates, carob powder, and vanilla extract, and continue processing until the mixture forms a small ball. Transfer to a cake plate or round serving platter, and form into an 8-inch round torte.

Icing

½ cup	cashews, soaked 1 hour
¼ cup	pine nuts, soaked 1 hour
3 tablespoons	agave nectar
2 tablespoons	raw almond butter
2 tablespoons	raw carob powder
1 teaspoon	vanilla extract

Combine all the ingredients in a food processor fitted with the S blade, or in a blender, and process until smooth, thick, and creamy. Add a small amount of water, as needed, to achieve the desired consistency. Spread the icing over the top of the torte.

Decoration for the Sides

½ cup   finely chopped walnuts

Press the finely chopped walnuts evenly on all sides of the torte. Refrigerate the torte for 2–3 hours before serving.

Fig Torte

Yield: 8–10 servings

Torte

2 cups	Brazil nuts, soaked 1 hour
2 cups	dried Black Mission figs
1 teaspoon	vanilla extract

*P*lace the Brazil nuts in a food processor fitted with the S blade, and process into a fine meal. Gradually add the figs and vanilla extract, and continue processing until the mixture forms a small ball. Transfer to a cake plate or round serving platter, and form into an 8-inch round torte.

Icing

1/2 cup	macadamia nuts or cashews, soaked 1 hour
1/4 cup	pine nuts, soaked 1 hour
3 tablespoons	agave nectar
1 teaspoon	vanilla extract

Combine all the ingredients in a food processor fitted with the S blade, or in a blender, and process until smooth, thick, and creamy. Add a small amount of water, as needed, to achieve the desired consistency. Spread the icing over the top of the torte.

Decoration for the Sides

       ½ cup   finely chopped walnuts

Press the finely chopped walnuts evenly on all sides of the torte.

Decorations for the Top

       3   kiwis, peeled and thinly sliced
      1 cup   fresh raspberries

Arrange the kiwi slices on top of the icing in a spiral, covering the entire torte and overlapping the slices slightly. Place the raspberries around the edges of the torte and some in the middle of the spiral. Refrigerate for 2–3 hours before serving.

Cakes

Banana Nut Carob Cake

Yield: 10–12 servings

Cake

3 cups	walnuts, soaked 1 hour
1½ cups	pitted dates
1½ cups	raisins
6 tablespoons	raw carob powder
2 teaspoons	vanilla extract

Place the walnuts in a food processor fitted with the S blade, and process into a fine meal. Gradually add the dates, raisins, carob powder, and vanilla extract, and continue processing until the mixture is smooth and forms a ball. Divide the mixture into 2 equal parts (for 2 layers), and form into the desired shape. Place the bottom layer of the cake on a cake plate or serving platter.

Icing

1 cup	macadamia nuts, soaked 1 hour
1 cup	cashews, soaked 1 hour
¼ cup	pine nuts, soaked 1 hour
1	large ripe banana
1 teaspoon	vanilla extract

Combine all the ingredients in a blender, and process until smooth, thick, and creamy. Add a small amount of water, as needed, to facilitate blending.

Filling

2   ripe bananas, thinly sliced

To assemble: Ice the first layer of cake, and layer the sliced bananas on top. Place the second layer of cake over the sliced bananas, and ice the top and sides of the cake with the remaining icing. Refrigerate for 2–3 hours before serving.

Almond Hazelnut Carob Torte

Yield: 8–10 servings

Torte

1 cup	almonds, soaked 12–48 hours
1 cup	hazelnuts, soaked 1 hour
1 cup	pitted medjool dates
1 cup	raisins
4 tablespoons	raw carob powder
1 teaspoon	vanilla extract

Place the almonds and hazelnuts in a food processor fitted with the S blade, and process into a fine meal. Gradually add the dates and raisins, carob powder, and vanilla extract, and continue processing until the mixture forms a small ball. Transfer to a cake plate or round serving platter, and form into an 8-inch round torte.

Icing

½ cup	macadamia nuts, soaked 1 hour
¼ cup	pine nuts, soaked 1 hour
3 tablespoons	agave nectar
3 tablespoons	raw carob powder
1 teaspoon	vanilla extract

Combine all the ingredients in a food processor fitted with the S blade, or in a blender, and process until smooth, thick, and creamy. Add a small amount of water, as needed, to achieve the desired consistency. Spread the icing over the top of the torte.

Decoration for the Sides

½ cup	finely chopped walnuts

Press the finely chopped walnuts evenly on all sides of the torte. Refrigerate the torte for 2–3 hours before serving.

Cakes

Magical Blueberry Cake

Yield: 10–12 servings

Cake

3 cups	almonds, soaked 12–48 hours
1½ cups	pitted medjool dates
1½ cups	raisins
½ cup	raw carob powder
2 teaspoons	vanilla extract

*P*lace the almonds in a food processor fitted with the S blade, and process into a fine meal. Gradually add the dates, raisins, carob powder, and vanilla extract, and continue processing until the mixture is smooth and forms a ball. Divide the mixture into 2 equal parts (for 2 layers), and form into the desired shape. Place the bottom layer of the cake on a cake plate or serving platter.

Icing

2 cups	macadamia nuts or cashews, soaked 1 hour
1 cup	fresh or frozen blueberries
	Water or young coconut water, as needed

Combine the macadamia nuts and blueberries in a food processor fitted with the S blade, or in a blender, and process until smooth and creamy. Add a small amount of water or coconut water, as needed, to achieve the desired consistency. The icing should be smooth, thick, and creamy.

Filling

2	ripe bananas, thinly sliced
1/4 teaspoon	ground cinnamon

Decoration for the Top

Edible fresh flowers

To assemble: Ice the first layer of the cake, and top it with a layer of the thinly sliced bananas. Sprinkle the bananas lightly with cinnamon. Place the second layer of the cake on top of the bananas, and ice the whole cake. Decorate with edible fresh flowers. Refrigerate for 2–3 hours before serving.

Cakes

Heavenly Apricot Torte

Yield: 8–10 servings

Torte

1 cup	almonds, soaked 12–48 hours
1 cup	pecans, soaked 1 hour
1 cup	pitted medjool dates
1 cup	raisins
1 teaspoon	vanilla extract

Combine the almonds and pecans in a food processor fitted with the S blade, and process into a fine meal. Gradually add the dates, raisins, and vanilla extract, and process until the mixture is smooth and forms a ball. Transfer to a cake plate or round serving platter, and form into an 8-inch round torte approximately 1 inch high.

Icing

1 cup	dried Turkish apricots, soaked 1 hour
1/4 cup	pine nuts, soaked 1 hour
1/4 teaspoon	ground cinnamon
1/4 teaspoon	ground coriander

Combine all the ingredients in a food processor fitted with the S blade, or in a blender, and process until smooth, thick, and creamy. Add a small amount of water, as needed, to achieve the desired consistency. Spread the icing over the torte.

Decoration for the Sides

      ½ cup   finely chopped hazelnuts

Press the finely chopped hazelnuts evenly on all sides of the torte. Refrigerate the torte for 2–3 hours before serving.

Cakes

Spice Cake with Pears and Raisin Sauce

Yield: 10–12 servings

Cake

3 cups	almonds, soaked 12–48 hours
3 cups	pitted medjool dates
1 teaspoon	ground cinnamon
1/4 teaspoon	ground cloves
1/4 teaspoon	ground coriander
1/4 teaspoon	ground nutmeg

Place the almonds in a food processor fitted with the S blade, and process into a fine meal. Gradually add the dates, cinnamon, cloves, coriander, and nutmeg, and continue processing until the mixture forms a small ball. Transfer to a cake plate or round serving platter, and form into a 9-inch round cake.

Raisin Sauce

1/2 cup	raisins, soaked 2 hours
1/2 cup	young coconut pulp

Combine the raisins and coconut pulp in a blender, and process until smooth, thick, and creamy. Add a small amount of water, as needed, to achieve the desired consistency. Spread the sauce evenly on top of the cake.

Decorations for the Top

3	pears, peeled and thinly sliced
3	small edible fresh flowers

Arrange the sliced pears on top of the raisin sauce in a spiral, covering the entire cake and overlapping the slices slightly. Place the flowers in the center of the spiral. Refrigerate for 2–3 hours before serving.

Decadent Chocolate Torte

See photo facing this page.

Yield: 8–10 servings

Torte

2 cups	pecans, soaked 1 hour
2 cups	pitted medjool dates
4 tablespoons	raw cacao nibs, ground superfine
1 teaspoon	vanilla extract

Place the pecans in a food processor fitted with the S blade, and process into a fine meal. Gradually add the dates, cacao nibs, and vanilla extract, and continue processing until the mixture forms a small ball. Transfer to a cake plate or round serving platter, and form into an 8-inch round torte.

Icing

½ cup	macadamia nuts or cashews, soaked 1 hour
¼ cup	pine nuts, soaked 1 hour
3 tablespoons	agave nectar
2 tablespoons	raw cacao nibs, ground superfine
1 teaspoon	vanilla extract

Decadent Chocolate Torte, 32–33

Combine all the ingredients in a food processor fitted with the S blade, or in a blender, and process until smooth, thick, and creamy. Add a small amount of water, as needed, to achieve the desired consistency. Spread the icing over the top of the torte.

Decorations for the Sides and Top

½ cup	finely chopped hazelnuts
	Edible fresh flowers or fruit
	Mint leaves

Press the hazelnuts evenly on all sides of the torte. Decorate the top of the torte with fresh flowers or fruit, and accent it with a few fresh mint leaves. Refrigerate the torte for 2–3 hours before serving.

Magical Truffles, 44

Cakes

Persimmon Torte

Yield: 8–10 servings

Torte

2 cups	walnuts, soaked 1 hour
2 cups	pitted medjool dates
1/2 teaspoon	ground allspice

Place the walnuts in a food processor fitted with the S blade, and process into a fine meal. Gradually add the dates and allspice, and process until the mixture forms a small ball. Transfer to a cake plate or round serving platter, and form into an 8-inch round torte.

Icing

1/2 cup	macadamia nuts or cashews, soaked 1 hour
1/2 cup	ripe persimmon pulp
1/2 teaspoon	vanilla extract

Combine all the ingredients in a blender, and process until smooth, thick, and creamy. Add a small amount of water, as needed, to achieve the desired consistency. Spread the icing evenly over the torte.

Decoration for the Sides

1/2 cup	finely chopped hazelnuts

Press the hazelnuts evenly into the sides of the torte. Refrigerate the torte for 2–3 hours before serving.

Exotic Brazilian Cake

Yield: 8–10 servings

Cake

3 cups	Brazil nuts, soaked 1 hour
3 cups	pitted medjool dates
2 teaspoons	vanilla extract
1 teaspoon	ground cinnamon
1 teaspoon	ground ginger
1/4 teaspoon	ground allspice
1/4 teaspoon	ground cloves

*P*lace the Brazil nuts in a food processor fitted with the S blade, and process into a fine meal. Gradually add the dates, vanilla extract, cinnamon, ginger, allspice, and cloves, and continue processing until the mixture forms a ball. Divide the mixture into 2 equal parts (for 2 layers), and form each part into a round cake layer, about 8 inches in diameter. Place each layer on a plate.

Icing

1 cup	chopped fresh or frozen pineapple
3/4 cup	cashews, soaked 1 hour
3/4 cup	macadamia nuts, soaked 1 hour
1/4 cup	pine nuts, soaked 1 hour
1 teaspoon	vanilla extract

Combine all the ingredients in a food processor fitted with the S blade, or in a blender, and process until smooth, thick, and creamy. Add a small amount of water, as needed, to achieve the desired consistency. Ice the first layer of the cake. Place the second layer of the cake on top and ice the whole cake. Refrigerate for 2–3 hours before serving.

Cakes

Blueberry Cheesecake

Yield: 12–14 servings

Crust

2 cups	pecans, soaked 30 minutes
2 cups	pitted medjool dates
1/4 teaspoon	ground cinnamon

Place the pecans in a food processor fitted with the S blade, and process into a fine meal. Gradually add the dates and cinnamon, and process until the mixture forms a small ball. Press the mixture into an 8- or 9-inch springform pan to form the crust.

Cheesecake

4 cups	almonds, soaked 12–48 hours and blanched (see page 10)
1/4 cup	fresh lemon juice
2 cups	pitted medjool dates
1 teaspoon	almond extract
1 teaspoon	vanilla extract
1/4 teaspoon	Celtic salt

Combine the almonds and lemon juice in a blender, and process until smooth and creamy. Add a small amount of water, as needed, to achieve the desired consistency. Pour into a juice bag and squeeze out the liquid until the pulp is a moist pâté. Transfer to a food processor fitted with the S blade. Add the remaining ingredients, and process until smooth and well combined. Spread on top of the crust, and pat until firm. Refrigerate for 2–3 hours before serving.

Topping

2 cups	fresh or frozen blueberries
¼ cup	pitted dates, soaked 1 hour

Combine the blueberries and dates in a food processor fitted with the S blade, or in a blender, and process until smooth. Spoon 2–3 tablespoons on top of each serving of cheesecake.

Incredibly Decadent Chocolate Cake

Yield: 8–10 servings

Cake

2 cups	almonds, soaked 12–48 hours and dehydrated 18 hours
2 cups	pitted medjool dates
⅓ cup	raw almond butter
4 tablespoons	raw cacao nibs, ground superfine
4 tablespoons	agave nectar
2 teaspoons	vanilla extract

*P*lace the almonds in a food processor fitted with the S blade, and process into a fine meal. Gradually add the dates, almond butter, cacao nibs, agave nectar, and vanilla extract, and continue processing until the mixture is well blended and forms a ball. If you have difficulty getting the mixture to blend, add a small amount of water, as needed, to facilitate blending and achieve the desired consistency. Divide the mixture into 2 equal parts (for 2 layers), and form each part into a round cake layer, about 8 inches in diameter. Place each layer on a plate.

Filling

2	large ripe bananas, thinly sliced

Arrange the sliced bananas on top of the bottom layer, and place the second layer on top of the bananas.

Icing

1	ripe avocado
1	ripe banana
5	pitted medjool dates
½ cup	water
⅓ cup	pine nuts, soaked 1 hour
2 tablespoons	raw cacao nibs, ground superfine
1 teaspoon	vanilla extract

Combine all the ingredients in a blender, and process until smooth, thick, and creamy. Ice the top and sides of the cake.

Decoration for the Top

1 pint	strawberries, stems removed and thinly sliced

Arrange the strawberries on the top of the cake in a spiral, covering the entire cake and overlapping slightly. Refrigerate the cake for 2–3 hours before serving.

Raspberry Torte

Yield: 6–8 servings

Torte

2 cups	Brazil nuts, soaked 1 hour
2 cups	pitted medjool dates
1 teaspoon	vanilla extract

Place the Brazil nuts in a food processor fitted with the S blade, and process into a fine meal. Gradually add the dates and vanilla extract, and continue processing until the mixture forms a ball. Transfer to a cake plate or round serving platter, and form into an 8-inch round torte.

Icing

½ cup	macadamia nuts or cashews, soaked 1 hour
¼ cup	pine nuts, soaked 1 hour
¼ cup	fresh or frozen raspberries
2 tablespoons	agave nectar
1 teaspoon	vanilla extract
	Young coconut water or water, as needed

Combine the macadamia nuts, pine nuts, raspberries, agave nectar, and vanilla extract in a blender, and process until smooth, thick, and creamy. Add a small amount of coconut water or water, as needed, to achieve the desired consistency. Spread the icing evenly over the torte.

Decoration for the Sides

1/2 cup   finely chopped hazelnuts

Press the chopped hazelnuts evenly into the sides of the torte. Refrigerate the torte for 2–3 hours before serving.

Decoration for the Edges

1 cup   fresh raspberries

Place the raspberries around the outer edges of the torte.

Lemon Cake

Cake

3 cups	almonds, soaked 12–48 hours
3 cups	pitted medjool dates
3 tablespoons	fresh lemon juice

Place the almonds in a food processor fitted with the S blade, and process into a fine meal. Gradually add the dates and lemon juice, and continue processing until the mixture forms a ball. Divide the mixture into 2 equal parts (for 2 layers), and form each part into a round cake layer, about 8 inches in diameter. Place each layer on a plate.

Icing

1$\frac{1}{2}$ cups	macadamia nuts or cashews, soaked 1 hour
$\frac{1}{2}$ cup	pine nuts, soaked 1 hour
4 tablespoons	fresh lemon juice
3 tablespoons	agave nectar
1 teaspoon	vanilla extract

Combine all the ingredients in a blender, and process until smooth, thick, and creamy. Add a small amount of water, as needed, to achieve the desired consistency. Ice the first layer of the cake. Place the second layer of the cake on top of the first layer, and ice the whole cake. Refrigerate for 2–3 hours before serving.

Candies and Truffles

Persimmon Candy

This recipe is simple but delicious. It tastes just like candy, and makes a great snack for when you go hiking.

20	ripe persimmons

Slice the persimmons into ¼-inch-thick pieces. Place on a dehydrator tray and dehydrate at 105 degrees for 16–18 hours, or until the persimmons are completely dry. Store the dried persimmons in an airtight glass container at room temperature.

Magical Truffles

See photo facing page 33.   *Yield:* 30 truffles

2 cups	pecans, soaked 1 hour
2 cups	dried Turkish apricots
1 teaspoon	vanilla extract
¼ teaspoon	ground coriander
	Unsweetened shredded dried coconut

Place the pecans in a food processor fitted with the S blade, and process into a fine meal. Gradually add the apricots, vanilla extract, and coriander, and continue processing until the mixture forms a ball. Form into ¾-inch balls, and roll them in shredded coconut until evenly coated all over.

Banana Chips

10	large ripe bananas

Slice the bananas into ¼-inch pieces. Place on a dehydrator tray and dehydrate at 105 degrees for 16–18 hours, or until the bananas are completely dry. Store the dried bananas in an airtight glass container at room temperature.

Cherry Truffles

Yield: 30 truffles

1½ cups	pecans, soaked 1 hour
½ cup	pine nuts, soaked 1 hour
2 cups	pitted medjool dates
1 teaspoon	vanilla extract
30	dried cherries
	Unsweetened shredded dried coconut

Combine the pecans and pine nuts in a food processor fitted with the S blade, and process into a fine meal. Gradually add the dates and vanilla extract, and continue processing until the mixture forms a ball. Form into ¾-inch balls, and place a dried cherry in the middle. Roll the balls in shredded coconut until evenly coated all over.

Outrageous Fudge

2 cups	pecans, soaked 30 minutes
1 cup	pine nuts, soaked 30 minutes
1½ cups	pitted medjool dates
¾ cup	raw carob powder
2 teaspoons	vanilla extract
1½ cups	walnuts, soaked 1 hour and chopped

Combine the pecans and pine nuts in a food processor fitted with the S blade, and process into a fine meal. Gradually add the dates, carob powder, and vanilla extract, and continue processing until the mixture forms a ball. Transfer to a bowl, and stir in the chopped walnuts. Mix well. Spread the mixture evenly in an 8 x 8-inch glass dish. Score the fudge into 1-inch squares. Cover and store in the freezer. Serve cold.

Sweet Nut and Seed Bliss Balls

Yield: 16 balls

1/2 cup	almonds, soaked 12–48 hours
1/2 cup	hazelnuts, soaked 1 hour
1/2 cup	pecans, soaked 1 hour
1/2 cup	pumpkin seeds, soaked 4 hours
1/2 cup	sunflower seeds, soaked 4 hours
1/4 cup	pine nuts, soaked 1 hour
1 cup	chopped medjool dates
4 tablespoons	raw carob powder
3 tablespoons	raw tahini
2/3 cup	unsweetened shredded dried coconut

Combine the almonds, hazelnuts, pecans, pumpkin seeds, sunflower seeds, pine nuts, and dates in a food processor fitted with the S blade, and process until all the nuts and seeds are chunky. Transfer to a large bowl, and add the carob powder and tahini. Mix well. Form into balls, about 1 1/2 inches in diameter, and roll in the shredded coconut until evenly coated all over. Store the balls in the refrigerator.

Angelic Balls

Yield: 16 balls

1 cup	almonds, soaked 12–48 hours
1 cup	pecans, soaked 1 hour
½ cup	chopped medjool dates
½ cup	dried Turkish apricots
¼ cup	pine nuts, soaked 1 hour
3 tablespoons	raw almond butter
1 teaspoon	ground cardamom
1 teaspoon	ground coriander
1 teaspoon	vanilla extract
⅔ cup	unsweetened shredded dried coconut

Combine the almonds, pecans, dates, apricots, and pine nuts in a food processor fitted with the S blade, and process until chunky. Transfer to a large bowl, and add the almond butter, cardamom, coriander, and vanilla extract. Mix well. Form into balls, about 1½ inches in diameter, and roll in the shredded coconut until evenly coated all over. Store the balls in the refrigerator.

Divine Heavenly Truffles

Yield: 30 truffles

1 cup	almonds, soaked 12–48 hours
½ cup	pine nuts, soaked 1 hour
1 cup	pitted medjool dates
½ cup	raisins
¼ cup	raw carob powder
1 teaspoon	vanilla extract
¼ teaspoon	peppermint extract
	Unsweetened shredded dried coconut

Combine the almonds and pine nuts in a food processor fitted with the S blade, and process into a fine meal. Gradually add the dates, raisins, carob powder, vanilla extract, and peppermint extract, and continue processing until the mixture forms a ball. Form into ¾-inch balls, and roll them in shredded coconut until evenly coated all over. Store the truffles in the refrigerator.

Candies and Truffles

Exotic Spice Truffles

Yield: 24 truffles

1½ cups	almonds, soaked 12–48 hours
¾ cup	pitted medjool dates
¾ cup	raisins
½ teaspoon	ground cinnamon
⅛ teaspoon	ground nutmeg
⅛ teaspoon	ground cloves
⅛ teaspoon	ground coriander
	Unsweetened shredded dried coconut

Place the almonds in a food processor fitted with the S blade, and process into a fine meal. Gradually add the dates, raisins, cinnamon, nutmeg, cloves, and coriander, and continue processing until the mixture forms a ball. Form into ¾-inch balls, and roll them in shredded coconut until evenly coated all over. Store the truffles in the refrigerator.

Cookies
and Bars

Jam Jewels

See photo facing page 64.

Yield: 35 *cookies*

Cookie Dough

2 cups	almonds, soaked 12–48 hours
1	apple, cored and chopped
1/2 cup	pitted dates
2 tablespoons	golden flaxseeds, ground superfine
1 teaspoon	ground cinnamon
1 teaspoon	vanilla extract
1/2 teaspoon	Celtic salt
1/4 teaspoon	ground cardamom
1/4 teaspoon	ground coriander

Process the almonds, apple, and dates through a Champion Juicer fitted with the solid plate. Transfer to a bowl, and stir in the flaxseeds, cinnamon, vanilla extract, salt, cardamom, and coriander. Mix well.

Fruit Filling

½ *cup*	dried Turkish apricots, soaked 1 hour
2 *tablespoons*	water

Combine the apricots and water in a blender, and process until smooth.

To assemble: Form the cookie dough into 1-inch balls. Using your thumb or index finger, make a depression in the center of each cookie. Fill the depression with some of the fruit filling. Place on a dehydrator tray and dehydrate at 105 degrees for 8–10 hours, or until the desired crispness is achieved.

Apricot Cookies

2 cups	sunflower seeds, soaked 4–6 hours
1 cup	dried Turkish apricots, soaked 1 hour
1	apple, cored and chopped
1 cup	pecans, soaked 1 hour and chopped
1 teaspoon	vanilla extract
1/2 teaspoon	ground cinnamon
1/8 teaspoon	ground nutmeg
1/8 teaspoon	ground cloves
1/8 teaspoon	ground coriander

Process the sunflower seeds, apricots, and apple through a Champion Juicer fitted with the solid plate, or in a food processor fitted with the S blade. Transfer to a bowl, and add the pecans, vanilla extract, cinnamon, nutmeg, cloves, and coriander. Mix well. Form into cookies about $1\frac{1}{2}$ inches in diameter and about $\frac{1}{2}$ inch thick, and place on a dehydrator tray with a Teflex sheet. Dehydrate at 105 degrees for 6 hours. Turn the cookies over and remove the Teflex sheet. Continue dehydrating for 6 hours, or until the desired crispness is achieved.

Apple Banana Pecan Cookies

2 cups	sunflower seeds, soaked 4–6 hours
2	ripe bananas
1	sweet apple, cored and chopped
1/2 cup	pitted dates
1/2 cup	young coconut water or water
1 cup	pecans, soaked 1 hour and chopped
3 tablespoons	golden flaxseeds, ground superfine
1 teaspoon	ground cinnamon
1 teaspoon	Celtic salt
1 teaspoon	vanilla extract

Combine the sunflower seeds, bananas, apple, dates, and coconut water in a blender, and process until smooth and thick. Transfer to a large bowl, and add the pecans, flaxseeds, cinnamon, salt, and vanilla extract. Mix well. Spoon the dough onto a dehydrator tray with a Teflex sheet, and form into small cookies, about 1½ inches in diameter and ½ inch thick. Dehydrate at 105 degrees for 4–6 hours. Turn the cookies over and remove the Teflex sheet. Continue dehydrating for 9–10 hours, or until the cookies are dry on the outside and slightly moist on the inside.

Fudge Brownies Supreme

See photo between pages 64-65.

Yield: 25–30 *brownies*

2 cups	sunflower seeds, soaked 4–6 hours
½ cup	pine nuts, soaked 1 hour
½ cup	pitted medjool dates
¼ cup	raw carob powder
1	apple, cored and grated
1 cup	pecans, soaked 1 hour and chopped
2 tablespoons	golden flaxseeds, ground superfine
1 teaspoon	Celtic salt
1 teaspoon	vanilla extract

Combine the sunflower seeds and pine nuts in a food processor fitted with the S blade, and process into a fine meal. Gradually add the dates and carob powder, and continue processing until well blended. Transfer to a bowl, and stir in the apple, pecans, flaxseeds, salt, and vanilla extract. Mix well. Form into 1½-inch squares, about ½ inch thick. Place on a dehydrator tray, and dehydrate at 105 degrees for 12–14 hours, or until the brownies are crispy on the outside and slightly moist inside. Cool before icing.

Icing

¼ *cup*	pine nuts, soaked 1 hour
¼ *cup*	raw carob powder
2 tablespoons	raw almond butter
2 tablespoons	agave nectar
1 teaspoon	vanilla extract

Combine all the ingredients in a blender, and process until smooth, thick, and creamy. Add a small amount of water, as needed, to achieve the desired consistency. Chill in the refrigerator before icing the brownies.

Persimmon Cookies

2 cups	sunflower seeds, soaked 6–8 hours
1½ cups	chopped ripe persimmons
½ cup	young coconut water or water
¼ cup	pitted dates, soaked 1 hour
1 cup	raisins
1 cup	walnuts, soaked 1 hour and finely chopped
1	apple, cored and grated
2 tablespoons	golden flaxseeds, ground superfine
1 teaspoon	ground cinnamon
1 teaspoon	vanilla extract
½ teaspoon	Celtic salt

Combine the sunflower seeds, persimmons, coconut water, and dates in a blender, and process until smooth and thick. Transfer to a large bowl, and add the raisins, walnuts, apple, flaxseeds, cinnamon, vanilla extract, and salt. Mix well. Spoon the dough onto a dehydrator tray with a Teflex sheet, and form into small cookies, about 1½ inches in diameter and ½ inch thick. Dehydrate at 105 degrees for 4–6 hours. Turn the cookies over and remove the Teflex sheet. Continue dehydrating for 9–10 hours, or until the cookies are dry on the outside and slightly moist on the inside.

Hazelnut Spice Cookies

Yield: 24 cookies

2 cups	hazelnuts, soaked 1 hour
2 cups	raisins
1 tablespoon	pumpkin pie spice
1 teaspoon	vanilla extract
1 cup	unsweetened shredded dried coconut

Place the hazelnuts in a food processor fitted with the S blade, and process into a fine meal. Gradually add the raisins, pumpkin pie spice, and vanilla extract. Process until thoroughly blended. Form into cookies, about $1\frac{1}{2}$ inches in diameter and $\frac{1}{4}$ inch thick. Carefully roll in the shredded coconut until evenly coated all over. Store the cookies in a glass container in the refrigerator.

Pineapple Raisin Nut Bars

See photo facing page 64.

Yield: 16 bars

Bottom Layer

2¹⁄₂ cups	hazelnuts, soaked 1 hour
2¹⁄₂ cups	unsweetened shredded dried coconut
¹⁄₄ cup	medjool dates
1 tablespoon	raw coconut oil
1 teaspoon	lemon extract, or 1 tablespoon fresh lemon juice
¹⁄₄ teaspoon	Celtic salt

*P*lace the hazelnuts in a food processor fitted with the S blade, and process into a fine meal. Gradually add the dried coconut, dates, coconut oil, lemon extract, and salt, and process until well blended. Press firmly into an 8 x 8-inch glass dish.

Top Layer

³⁄₄ cup	raisins
¹⁄₂ cup	macadamia nuts
¹⁄₂ cup	chopped dried pineapple
2 tablespoons	agave nectar

Combine the raisins, macadamia nuts, and pineapple in a food processor fitted with the S blade, and pulse until chunky. Add the agave nectar and mix well. Lightly press the nut and fruit mixture into the bottom layer. Refrigerate for 2–3 hours before serving.

Berry Brazil Nut Bars

Yield: 16 bars

Bottom Layer

2½ cups	Brazil nuts, soaked 1 hour
2½ cups	unsweetened shredded dried coconut
1 tablespoon	raw coconut oil
1 teaspoon	vanilla extract
¼ teaspoon	Celtic salt

Place the Brazil nuts in a food processor fitted with the S blade, and process into a fine meal. Gradually add the dried coconut, coconut oil, vanilla extract, and salt, and process until well blended. Press firmly into an 8 x 8-inch glass dish.

Top Layer

¾ cup	macadamia nuts
¾ cup	dried blackberries, strawberries, or raspberries
½ cup	medjool dates
2 tablespoons	agave nectar

Combine the macadamia nuts, berries, and dates in a food processor fitted with the S blade, and pulse until chunky. Add the agave nectar and mix well. Lightly press the nut and fruit mixture into the bottom layer. Refrigerate for 2–3 hours before serving.

Cranberry Walnut Oatmeal Cookies

Yield: 30 cookies

2 cups	oat groats, soaked 12 hours
¾ cup	water
½ cup	pitted dates, soaked 1 hour
2	apples, cored and grated
1 cup	dried cranberries, soaked 1 hour
1 cup	walnuts, soaked 1 hour and chopped
½ cup	raisins
1½ teaspoons	ground cinnamon
1 teaspoon	vanilla extract
½ teaspoon	Celtic salt
⅛ teaspoon	ground nutmeg

Combine the oat groats, water, and dates in a food processor fitted with the S blade, or in a blender, and process until thoroughly blended. Transfer to a bowl, and stir in the apples, cranberries, walnuts, raisins, cinnamon, vanilla extract, salt, and nutmeg. Mix well. Spoon the dough onto a dehydrator tray with a Teflex sheet, and form into small cookies, about 1½ inches in diameter and ½ inch thick. Dehydrate at 105 degrees for 6 hours. Turn the cookies over and remove the Teflex sheet. Continue dehydrating for 12–14 hours, or until the cookies are dry on the outside and slightly moist on the inside.

Heavenly Apricot Nut Bars

Yield: 16 bars

Bottom Layer

2½ cups	almonds, soaked 12–48 hours and dehydrated 18 hours
2½ cups	unsweetened shredded dried coconut
2 teaspoons	ground cinnamon
1 teaspoon	vanilla extract
¼ teaspoon	Celtic salt

Place the almonds in a food processor fitted with the S blade, and process into a fine meal. Gradually add the coconut, cinnamon, vanilla extract, and salt, and process until well combined. Press firmly into an 8 x 8-inch glass dish.

Top Layer

½ cup	chopped cashews
½ cup	raisins
½ cup	finely chopped dried Turkish apricots
2 tablespoons	agave nectar
1 tablespoon	unsweetened shredded dried coconut

Combine all the ingredients in a bowl, and mix well. Lightly press the nut and fruit mixture into the bottom layer. Refrigerate for 2–3 hours before serving.

Cookies and Bars

Brazil Nut Cookies

Yield: 24 cookies

2 cups	Brazil nuts, soaked 1 hour
2 cups	dried Black Mission figs
1/2 teaspoon	ground cinnamon
1/8 teaspoon	ground nutmeg
1/8 teaspoon	ground cloves
1/8 teaspoon	ground coriander
	Unsweetened shredded dried coconut

Place the Brazil nuts in a food processor fitted with the S blade, and process into a fine meal. Gradually add the figs, cinnamon, nutmeg, cloves, and coriander. Process until thoroughly blended. Form into cookies, about 1½ inches in diameter and ¼ inch thick. Roll in shredded coconut until evenly coated all over. Store the cookies in a glass container in the refrigerator.

Jam Jewels, 52–53, Pineapple Raisin Nut Bars, 60

next photo: Brownies Supreme, Fudge, 56–57

Snickerdoodles

Yield: 25 cookies

2 cups	almonds, soaked 12–48 hours and blanched (see page 10)
1	apple, peeled, cored, and chopped
1 cup	pitted dates, soaked 15 minutes
1 teaspoon	vanilla extract
½ teaspoon	Celtic salt
¼ cup	raw sugar
1 tablespoon	ground cinnamon

Process the almonds, apple, and dates through a Champion Juicer fitted with the solid plate, or through a Green Power Juicer. Add the vanilla extract and salt, and mix well. Spoon the dough onto a dehydrator tray and form into cookies, about 2 inches in diameter and ¼ inch thick. Sprinkle the cookies with the raw sugar and cinnamon, and dehydrate at 105 degrees for 14–16 hours, or until the desired crispness is achieved.

Cranberry Orange Nut Bread, 80

previous photo: Strawberry Mousse, 95

Raisin Date Hazelnut Bars

Bottom Layer

2¹/2 cups	hazelnuts, soaked 1 hour
2¹/2 cups	unsweetened shredded dried coconut
1 tablespoon	raw coconut oil
1 teaspoon	vanilla extract
1/2 teaspoon	ground cinnamon
1/4 teaspoon	Celtic salt
1/8 teaspoon	ground cloves
1/8 teaspoon	ground coriander
1/8 teaspoon	ground nutmeg

*P*lace the hazelnuts in a food processor fitted with the S blade, and process into a fine meal. Gradually add the remaining ingredients and process until well combined. Press firmly into an 8 x 8-inch glass dish.

Top Layer

3/4 cup	macadamia nuts
3/4 cup	raisins
1/2 cup	dried Black Mission figs
1/4 cup	pitted dates
2 tablespoons	agave nectar

Combine the macadamia nuts, raisins, figs, and dates in a food processor fitted with the S blade, and pulse until chunky. Add the agave nectar and mix well. Lightly press the nut and fruit mixture into the bottom layer. Refrigerate for 2–3 hours before serving.

Divine Nut Bars

Bottom Layer

1½ cups	almonds, soaked 12–48 hours and dehydrated 18 hours
1 cup	Brazil nuts
2½ cups	unsweetened shredded dried coconut
3	pitted medjool dates
1 tablespoon	raw coconut oil
1 teaspoon	ground cinnamon
1 teaspoon	vanilla extract

Combine the almonds and Brazil nuts in a food processor fitted with the S blade, and process into a fine meal. Gradually add the coconut, dates, coconut oil, cinnamon, and vanilla extract, and process until well combined. Press firmly into an 8 x 8-inch glass dish.

Top Layer

1 cup	pecans, soaked 30 minutes
1 cup	raisins
½ cup	almonds, soaked 12–48 hours and dehydrated 18 hours
4 tablespoons	agave nectar

Combine the pecans, raisins, and almonds in a food processor fitted with the S blade, and process until chunky. Transfer to a large bowl, and add the agave nectar. Stir until the nuts and raisins are coated evenly with the agave nectar. Lightly press the nut and fruit mixture into the bottom layer. Refrigerate for 2–3 hours before serving.

Dream Bars

Bottom Layer

1 cup	almonds, soaked 12–48 hours and dehydrated 18 hours
1 cup	unsweetened shredded dried coconut
2	pitted medjool dates
3 tablespoons	raw carob powder
2 teaspoons	raw coconut oil

Place the almonds in a food processor fitted with the S blade, and process into a fine meal. Gradually add the coconut, dates, carob powder, and coconut oil, and process until blended and moist. Press into an 8 x 8-inch glass dish.

Top Layer

1/2 cup	macadamia nuts
1/2 cup	raisins
1/4 cup	pine nuts
1 tablespoon	unsweetened shredded dried coconut
2 tablespoons	agave nectar

Combine the macadamia nuts, raisins, pine nuts, and coconut in a food processor fitted with the S blade, and pulse until chunky. Transfer to a large bowl, and add the agave nectar. Stir until the nuts and raisins are coated evenly with the agave nectar. Lightly press the nut and fruit mixture into the bottom layer. Refrigerate for 2–3 hours before serving.

Living in the Raw

Dessert Breads

The secret to making great bread is in grinding the flaxseeds. Grind the flaxseeds in a coffee grinder or blender. Do not grind the flaxseeds superfine; keep them somewhat coarse and chunky. The bread should be dry and crispy on the outside and slightly moist on the inside. You may need to adjust the time required for dehydrating depending on the weather, the amount of moisture in the ingredients, and your own personal preference. If the dough is dry and crumbly and has difficulty holding together, add a small amount of water.

Store the bread in an airtight glass container, either at room temperature or in the refrigerator. The bread will keep for approximately seven days.

Persimmon Nut Bread

Yield: 3 loaves, 30 servings

1 cup	pecans, soaked 1 hour
2 cups	golden flaxseeds, coarsely ground
1 cup	very ripe persimmon pulp
1/2 cup	raisins
1/2 cup	walnuts, soaked 1 hour and chopped
1	apple, cored and grated
1 teaspoon	Celtic salt
1 teaspoon	ground cinnamon
1 teaspoon	vanilla extract

*P*lace the pecans in a food processor fitted with the S blade, and process into a fine meal. Transfer to a large bowl, and stir in the flaxseeds, persimmon pulp, raisins, walnuts, apple, salt, cinnamon, and vanilla extract. Mix well. Form into 3 loaves, each about 4 x 7 x ¾ inches, and dehydrate at 105 degrees for 12–14 hours, or until dry and crispy on the outside and slightly moist on the inside.

Holiday Nut Bread

Yield: 3 loaves, 30 servings

1 cup	almonds, soaked 12–48 hours
2 cups	golden flaxseeds, coarsely ground
2	apples, cored and grated
1½ cups	fresh cranberries, coarsely chopped
¼ cup	raisins or currants
¼ cup	finely chopped dried pineapple
1½ teaspoons	ground cinnamon
1 teaspoon	Celtic salt
1 teaspoon	vanilla extract

*P*lace the almonds in a food processor fitted with the S blade, and process into a fine meal. Transfer to a large bowl, and stir in the flaxseeds, apples, cranberries, raisins, pineapple, cinnamon, salt, and vanilla extract. Mix well. Form into 3 loaves, each about 4 x 7 x ¾ inches, and dehydrate at 105 degrees for 12–14 hours, or until dry and crispy on the outside and slightly moist on the inside.

Spiced Tea Bread

Yield: 3 loaves, 30 servings

1 cup	almonds, soaked 12–48 hours
2 cups	golden flaxseeds, coarsely ground
½ cup	finely grated carrots
½ cup	grated zucchini
2	apples, cored and grated
2 teaspoons	ground cinnamon
1 teaspoon	Celtic salt
1 teaspoon	vanilla extract
½ teaspoon	ground nutmeg
¼ teaspoon	ground cardamom

Place the almonds in a food processor fitted with the S blade, and process into a fine meal. Transfer to a large bowl, and stir in the flaxseeds, carrots, zucchini, apples, cinnamon, salt, vanilla extract, nutmeg, and cardamom. Mix well. Form into 3 loaves, each about 4 x 7 x ¾ inches, and dehydrate at 105 degrees for 12–14 hours, or until dry and crispy on the outside and slightly moist on the inside.

Banana Apricot Bread

Yield: 3 loaves, 30 servings

1 cup	almonds, soaked 12–48 hours
3	ripe bananas
2 cups	golden flaxseeds, coarsely ground
1 cup	finely chopped dried Turkish apricots
1/2 cup	walnuts, soaked 1 hour and finely chopped
1 teaspoon	Celtic salt
1 teaspoon	ground cinnamon
1 teaspoon	vanilla extract

Place the almonds in a food processor fitted with the S blade, and process into a fine meal. Add the bananas, and process until they are blended with the almonds. Transfer to a large bowl, and stir in the flaxseeds, apricots, walnuts, salt, cinnamon, and vanilla extract. Mix well. Form into 3 loaves, each about 4 x 7 x 3/4 inches, and dehydrate at 105 degrees for 12–14 hours, or until dry and crispy on the outside and slightly moist on the inside.

Dessert Breads

Apricot Nut Bread

Yield: 3 *loaves,* 30 *servings*

1 cup	pecans, soaked 1 hour
2 cups	golden flaxseeds, coarsely ground
1 cup	dried Turkish apricots, soaked 1 hour and blended
1	apple, cored and grated
1 tablespoon	grated lemon zest
1 teaspoon	ground allspice
1 teaspoon	Celtic salt

Place the pecans in a food processor fitted with the S blade, and process into a fine meal. Transfer to a large bowl, and stir in the flaxseeds, apricots, apple, lemon zest, allspice, and salt. Mix well. Form into 3 loaves, each about 4 x 7 x ¾ inches, and dehydrate at 105 degrees for 12–14 hours, or until dry and crispy on the outside and slightly moist on the inside.

Pistachio Nut Bread

Yield: 3 loaves, 30 servings

1 cup	pecans, soaked 1 hour
2 cups	golden flaxseeds, coarsely ground
1 cup	pistachios, soaked 1 hour and chopped
2	apples, cored and grated
1 teaspoon	ground cinnamon
1 teaspoon	vanilla extract
¼ teaspoon	ground cloves
¼ teaspoon	ground coriander
¼ teaspoon	ground nutmeg

Place the pecans in a food processor fitted with the S blade, and process into a fine meal. Transfer to a large bowl, and stir in the flaxseeds, pistachios, apples, cinnamon, vanilla extract, cloves, coriander, and nutmeg. Mix well. Form into 3 loaves, each about 4 x 7 x ¾ inches, and dehydrate at 105 degrees for 12–14 hours, or until dry and crispy on the outside and slightly moist on the inside.

Dessert Breads

Cinnamon Pecan Raisin Walnut Bread

Yield: 3 loaves, 30 servings

1 cup	pecans, soaked 1 hour
2 cups	golden flaxseeds, coarsely ground
3/4 cup	raisins, soaked 1 hour
3/4 cup	walnuts, soaked 1 hour and finely chopped
2 teaspoons	ground cinnamon
1 teaspoon	vanilla extract

*P*lace the pecans in a food processor fitted with the S blade, and process into a fine meal. Transfer to a large bowl, and stir in the flaxseeds, raisins, walnuts, cinnamon, and vanilla extract. Mix well. Form into 3 loaves, each about 4 x 7 x 3/4 inches, and dehydrate at 105 degrees for 12–14 hours, or until dry and crispy on the outside and slightly moist on the inside.

Fig, Banana, and Brazil Nut Tea Bread

Yield: 3 loaves, 30 servings

1 cup	Brazil nuts, soaked 1 hour
2	ripe bananas
2 cups	golden flaxseeds, coarsely ground
1 cup	dried figs, finely chopped
1	apple, cored and grated
2 teaspoons	pumpkin pie spice
1 teaspoon	Celtic salt

*P*lace the Brazil nuts in a food processor fitted with the S blade, and process into a fine meal. Add the bananas, and process until they are blended with the nuts. Transfer to a large bowl, and stir in the flaxseeds, figs, apple, pumpkin pie spice, and salt. Mix well. Form into 3 loaves, each about 4 x 7 x ¾ inches, and dehydrate at 105 degrees for 12–14 hours, or until dry and crispy on the outside and slightly moist on the inside.

Dessert Breads

Cherry Pecan Bread

Yield: 3 loaves, 30 servings

1 cup	almonds, soaked 12–48 hours
2 cups	golden flaxseeds, coarsely ground
2 cups	dried cherries, soaked 3 hours
1 cup	pecans, soaked 1 hour and chopped
2	apples, cored and grated
2 teaspoons	ground cinnamon
1 teaspoon	Celtic salt
1 teaspoon	vanilla extract

*P*lace the almonds in a food processor fitted with the S blade, and process into a fine meal. Transfer to a large bowl, and stir in the flaxseeds, cherries, pecans, apples, cinnamon, salt, and vanilla extract. Mix well. Form into 3 loaves, each about 4 x 7 x ¾ inches, and dehydrate at 105 degrees for 12–14 hours, or until dry and crispy on the outside and slightly moist on the inside.

Mango and Ginger Nut Bread

Yield: 3 loaves, 30 servings

1 cup	almonds, soaked 12–48 hours
2 cups	golden flaxseeds, coarsely ground
1 cup	blended fresh or frozen mango
½ cup	finely chopped dried mango, soaked 1 hour
½ cup	finely chopped dried ginger
1	apple, cored and grated
1 teaspoon	Celtic salt
¼ teaspoon	ground nutmeg

Place the almonds in a food processor fitted with the S blade, and process into a fine meal. Transfer to a large bowl, and stir in the flaxseeds, fresh and dried mango, ginger, apple, salt, and nutmeg. Mix well. Form into 3 loaves, each about 4 x 7 x ¾ inches, and dehydrate at 105 degrees for 12–14 hours, or until dry and crispy on the outside and slightly moist on the inside.

Dessert Breads

Cranberry Orange Nut Bread

See photo facing page 65.

Yield: 3 loaves, 30 servings

1 cup	almonds, soaked 12–48 hours
2 cups	golden flaxseeds, coarsely ground
1 cup	dried cranberries, soaked 1 hour
1 cup	walnuts, soaked 1 hour and finely chopped
2	apples, cored and grated
¼ cup	fresh orange juice
2 tablespoons	grated orange zest
2 teaspoons	ground cinnamon
1 teaspoon	Celtic salt
1 teaspoon	vanilla extract

Place the almonds in a food processor fitted with the S blade, and process into a fine meal. Transfer to a large bowl, and stir in the flaxseeds, cranberries, walnuts, apples, orange juice, orange zest, cinnamon, salt, and vanilla extract. Mix well. Form into 3 loaves, each about 4 x 7 x ¾ inches, and dehydrate at 105 degrees for 12–14 hours, or until dry and crispy on the outside and slightly moist on the inside.

Banana Blueberry Bread

Yield: 3 loaves, 30 servings

1 cup	almonds, soaked 12–48 hours
3	ripe bananas
2 cups	golden flaxseeds, coarsely ground
1 cup	fresh blueberries, chopped, or ½ cup dried blueberries, soaked 1 hour
½ cup	walnuts, soaked 1 hour and finely chopped
1 teaspoon	Celtic salt
1 teaspoon	ground cinnamon
1 teaspoon	vanilla extract

Place the almonds in a food processor fitted with the S blade, and process into a fine meal. Add the bananas, and process until they are blended with the almonds. Transfer to a large bowl, and stir in the flaxseeds, blueberries, walnuts, salt, cinnamon, and vanilla extract. Mix well. Form into 3 loaves, each about 4 x 7 x ¾ inches, and dehydrate at 105 degrees for 12–14 hours, or until dry and crispy on the outside and slightly moist on the inside.

Dessert Breads

Ice Creams
and Sorbets

Almond Milk can be used to make a variety of ice creams and sorbets. A high-speed blender works best. I recommend a Vita-Mix or BlendTec Total Blender.

Almond Milk

2 *cups*	water
1½ *cups*	almonds, soaked 12–48 hours
2 *cups*	young coconut water
2 *teaspoons*	vanilla extract

Combine the water and almonds in a blender, and process until smooth. Strain through a piece of cheesecloth, a nut milk bag, or a clean nylon stocking. Stir in the coconut water and vanilla extract. Store Almond Milk in a glass container in the refrigerator.

Mango Sorbet

2 cups	coarsely chopped fresh mango
¼ cup	dried mango, soaked 1 hour
½ cup	young coconut water or soak water from the dried mango
1 teaspoon	vanilla extract

Combine all the ingredients in a blender, and process until smooth and creamy. Pour into 3 ice cube trays, and freeze for 8–12 hours. When ready to serve, process the cubes through a Champion Juicer fitted with the solid plate, or through a Green Power Juicer. Serve immediately in individual ice cream dishes.

Hazelnut Ice Cream

Yield: 4 *servings*

2 cups	water
1½ cups	hazelnuts, soaked 8 hours
2 cups	young coconut water
2 tablespoons	agave nectar
1 teaspoon	ground cinnamon
1 cup	fresh raspberries

Combine the water and hazelnuts in a blender, and process until smooth. Strain through a piece of cheesecloth, a nut milk bag, or a clean nylon stocking. Stir in the coconut water, agave nectar, and cinnamon. Pour into 3 ice cube trays, and freeze for 8–12 hours. When ready to serve, process the cubes through a Champion Juicer fitted with the solid plate, or through a Green Power Juicer. Serve immediately in individual ice cream dishes, and top with the fresh raspberries.

Variation

• To make a raspberry sauce, place the raspberries in a blender and process until smooth. Add a little young coconut water or water, as needed, to achieve the desired consistency. Serve over the Hazelnut Ice Cream.

Kulfi

1 quart	Almond Milk (page 84)
1 tablespoon	rose water
1 teaspoon	ground cardamom
1½ cups	pistachios, finely chopped
½ cup	golden raisins
2 tablespoons	dried cherries, cut in half

Combine the Almond Milk, rose water, and cardamom in a pitcher, and mix well. Pour into 3 ice cube trays, and freeze for 8–12 hours. When ready to serve, process the cubes through a Champion Juicer fitted with the solid plate, or through a Green Power Juicer. Serve immediately in individual ice cream dishes. Sprinkle the pistachios, raisins, and cherries over each serving.

Persimmon Ice Cream

2 cups	very ripe persimmons
1 cup	macadamia nuts or cashews, soaked 1 hour
1 cup	young coconut water or water
3	pitted medjool dates, soaked 1 hour
1 teaspoon	vanilla extract
1/2 teaspoon	ground cinnamon

Combine all the ingredients in a blender, and process until smooth and creamy. Pour into 3 ice cube trays, and freeze for 8–12 hours. When ready to serve, process the cubes through a Champion Juicer fitted with the solid plate, or through a Green Power Juicer. Serve immediately in individual ice cream dishes.

Living in the Raw 88

Banana Coconut Ice Cream

Yield: 4–6 servings

2	large ripe bananas
1 cup	young coconut pulp
1 cup	young coconut water
½ cup	pine nuts, soaked 1 hour
1 teaspoon	vanilla extract

Combine all the ingredients in a blender, and process until smooth and creamy. Pour into 3 ice cube trays, and freeze for 8–12 hours. When ready to serve, process the cubes through a Champion Juicer fitted with the solid plate, or through a Green Power Juicer. Serve immediately in individual ice cream dishes.

Carob Ice Cream with Raspberries

Yield: 4 servings

1 quart	Almond Milk (page 84)
2 cups	young coconut pulp
½ cup	raw carob powder
3 tablespoons	agave nectar
1 teaspoon	vanilla extract
1 cup	fresh raspberries

Combine the Almond Milk, coconut pulp, carob powder, agave nectar, and vanilla extract in a blender, and process until smooth. Pour into 3 ice cube trays, and freeze for 8–12 hours. When ready to serve, process the cubes through a Champion Juicer fitted with the solid plate, or through a Green Power Juicer. Serve immediately in individual ice cream dishes, and top with the fresh raspberries.

Puddings, Parfaits, and Mousses

Carob Mousse

1½ cups	fresh Black Mission figs
1 cup	pecans, soaked 1 hour
1 cup	young coconut pulp
¼ cup	pitted dates, soaked 1 hour
3 tablespoons	raw carob powder
1 teaspoon	vanilla extract
½ teaspoon	ground cinnamon
	Young coconut water, as needed

Combine all the ingredients in a blender, and process until smooth, thick, and creamy, adding just enough coconut water to facilitate blending. Refrigerate for 2 hours before serving.

Variation

• Serve with 1 cup sliced strawberries.

Persimmon Pudding

Yield: 4–6 servings

2 cups	very ripe persimmon pulp
1 cup	macadamia nuts or cashews, soaked 1 hour
1 cup	young coconut pulp
⅛ teaspoon	ground allspice
	Young coconut water, as needed

Combine all the ingredients in a blender, and process until smooth, thick, and creamy, adding just enough coconut water to facilitate blending. Refrigerate for 2 hours before serving.

Pineapple Parfait

2 cups	chopped fresh or frozen pineapple
1 cup	macadamia nuts or cashews, soaked 1 hour
1 cup	young coconut pulp
1 teaspoon	vanilla extract
2	ripe bananas, sliced

Combine the pineapple, macadamia nuts, coconut pulp, and vanilla extract in a blender, and process until smooth, thick, and creamy. Pour into parfait or wine glasses, layering the mixture with the sliced bananas.

Note

• For extra sweetness, add a few soaked dates while blending the pineapple mixture.

Strawberry Mousse

See photo between pages 64-65.

Yield: 4 *servings*

2 cups	fresh or frozen strawberries
2 cups	young coconut pulp
1/2 cup	macadamia nuts or cashews, soaked 1 hour
1/4 cup	pine nuts, soaked 1 hour
3	pitted medjool dates, soaked 1 hour
1 teaspoon	vanilla extract
	Young coconut water, as needed

Combine all the ingredients in a blender, and process until smooth, thick, and creamy, adding just enough coconut water to facilitate blending. Refrigerate for 2 hours before serving.

Variation

• Layer with fresh blueberries in parfait or wine glasses.

Raspberry Pudding Delight

Yield: 4–6 servings

2 cups	young coconut pulp
1½ cups	fresh or frozen raspberries
½ cup	macadamia nuts, soaked 1 hour
1 teaspoon	vanilla extract

Combine all the ingredients in a blender, and process until smooth, thick, and creamy. Refrigerate for 2 hours before serving.

Fourth of July Parfait, 102

Strawberry Parfait

Yield: 4 *servings*

2 *cups*	almonds, soaked 12–48 hours and blanched (see page 10)
½ *cup*	macadamia nuts, soaked 1 hour
½ *cup*	pine nuts, soaked 1 hour
½ *cup*	agave nectar
2 *teaspoons*	vanilla extract
1 *pint*	strawberries, stems removed and thinly sliced

To make a nut cream, combine the almonds, macadamia nuts, pine nuts, agave nectar, and vanilla extract in a blender, and process until smooth, thick, and creamy. Add water, as needed, to facilitate blending and achieve the desired consistency. Layer the strawberries and nut cream in clear goblets. Refrigerate for 2–3 hours before serving.

Piña Colada Pie, 114–115

Heavenly Rice Pudding

2 cups	young coconut pulp
1/2 cup	young coconut water
1/4 cup	pine nuts, soaked 1 hour
3	pitted medjool dates, soaked 1 hour
2	ripe bananas
1 teaspoon	ground cinnamon
1 teaspoon	vanilla extract
3/4 cup	wild rice, soaked 3–5 days until soft and fluffy

Combine the coconut pulp, coconut water, pine nuts, dates, bananas, cinnamon, and vanilla extract in a blender, and process until smooth, thick, and creamy. Transfer to a bowl, and stir in the wild rice. Mix well. Refrigerate for 2 hours before serving.

Blueberry Parfait

2 cups	young coconut pulp
1½ cups	fresh or frozen blueberries
½ cup	macadamia nuts or cashews, soaked 1 hour
¼ cup	pine nuts, soaked 1 hour
4	pitted medjool dates, soaked 1 hour
1 teaspoon	vanilla extract
2	ripe bananas, sliced

Combine the coconut pulp, blueberries, macadamia nuts, pine nuts, dates, and vanilla extract in a blender, and process until smooth, thick, and creamy. Layer with the sliced bananas in parfait or wine glasses. Refrigerate for 2 hours before serving.

Banana Pudding

2 cups	young coconut pulp
2	large ripe bananas
1 teaspoon	fresh lemon juice
1 teaspoon	vanilla extract

Combine the coconut pulp, bananas, lemon juice, and vanilla extract in a blender, and process until smooth, thick, and creamy. Refrigerate for 2 hours before serving.

Variation

• Layer with fresh fruit, such as blueberries, strawberries, raspberries, or mangoes.

Apricot Passion Pudding

Yield: 4 *servings*

2 cups	young coconut pulp
1½ cups	fresh apricots, or 1 cup dried Turkish apricots, soaked 1 hour
½ cup	macadamia nuts, soaked 1 hour
¼ cup	pine nuts, soaked 1 hour
1 teaspoon	vanilla extract
½ teaspoon	ground cinnamon
¼ teaspoon	ground coriander
⅔ cup	finely chopped fresh or frozen pineapple
1	large ripe banana, thinly sliced

Combine the coconut pulp, apricots, macadamia nuts, pine nuts, vanilla extract, cinnamon, and coriander in a blender, and process until smooth, thick, and creamy. Transfer to a bowl, add the pineapple and banana, and mix well. Refrigerate for 2 hours before serving.

Fourth of July Parfait

See photo facing page 96.

Yield: 4 servings

2 cups	almonds, soaked 12–48 hours and blanched (see page 10)
1 cup	cashews, soaked 1 hour
½ cup	agave nectar
2 teaspoons	vanilla extract
1 pint	blueberries
1 pint	raspberries

Combine the almonds, cashews, agave nectar, and vanilla extract in a blender, and process until smooth, thick, and creamy. Add water, as needed, to facilitate blending and achieve the desired consistency. Layer with the blueberries and raspberries in clear goblets. Refrigerate for 2–3 hours before serving.

Pies

Pumpkin Pie

Crust

2 cups	pecans, soaked 1 hour
2 cups	unsweetened shredded dried coconut
1 tablespoon	raw coconut oil

Place the pecans in a food processor fitted with the S blade, and process into a fine meal. Gradually add the dried coconut and coconut oil, and process until well blended. Press into a 9-inch glass pie plate.

Filling

¾ cup	almonds, soaked 12–48 hours and blanched (see page 10)
¾ cup	pitted dates, soaked 1 hour
¼ cup	pine nuts, soaked 1 hour
2½ cups	blended raw pumpkin pulp
1 teaspoon	ground cinnamon
1 teaspoon	vanilla extract
½ teaspoon	ground ginger
⅛ teaspoon	ground cloves

Process the almonds, dates, and pine nuts through a Champion Juicer fitted with the solid plate. Transfer to a large bowl, and stir in the pumpkin pulp. Add the cinnamon, vanilla extract, ginger, and cloves, and mix well. Spoon into the prepared crust. Refrigerate for 2–3 hours before serving.

Cream Topping

1 cup	cashews, soaked 1 hour
2 tablespoons	agave nectar

Combine the cashews and agave nectar in a blender, and process until smooth, thick, and creamy. Add a small amount of water, as needed, to facilitate blending and achieve the desired consistency. Refrigerate for 2–3 hours before serving. Place a dollop of the topping on each slice of Pumpkin Pie.

Key Lime Mango Crème Pie

Crust

2 cups	almonds, soaked 12–48 hours
1/2 cup	pitted medjool dates

*P*lace the almonds in a food processor fitted with the S blade, and process into a fine meal. Gradually add the dates, and process until well blended. Press into a 9-inch glass pie plate.

Bottom Layer

1	large ripe mango, sliced

Layer the sliced mango on the bottom of the prepared crust.

Filling

3 cups	young coconut pulp
1/2 cup	macadamia nuts or cashews, soaked 1 hour
1/3 cup	pitted dates, soaked 15 minutes
1/4 cup	coconut water
1/2	large ripe avocado
4 tablespoons	fresh lemon juice
4 tablespoons	fresh lime juice
1 tablespoon	agave nectar
1 tablespoon	psyllium powder
2 teaspoons	vanilla extract

Combine the coconut pulp, macadamia nuts, dates, and coconut water in a blender, and process until smooth, thick, and creamy. Add the avocado, lemon juice, lime juice, agave nectar, psyllium powder, and vanilla extract, and process until smooth. Pour the filling into the prepared crust, and refrigerate for 2–3 hours before serving.

Decoration for the Top

1	lime, sliced

Decorate the top of the pie with the lime slices.

Lemon Crème Pie

Yield: 6–8 servings

Crust

2 cups	Brazil nuts, soaked 1 hour
2 cups	unsweetened shredded dried coconut
1/2 cup	pitted dates
1 tablespoon	raw coconut oil
1 teaspoon	ground cinnamon
1/4 teaspoon	Celtic salt

Place the Brazil nuts in a food processor fitted with the S blade, and process into a fine meal. Gradually add the dried coconut, dates, coconut oil, cinnamon, and salt, and process until well blended. Add a small amount of water, as needed, to facilitate blending and achieve the desired consistency. Press into a 9-inch glass pie plate.

Filling

3 cups	young coconut pulp
1 cup	cashews, soaked 1 hour
1/2 cup	fresh lemon juice
1/2 cup	water
6 tablespoons	agave nectar

Combine the coconut pulp, cashews, lemon juice, water, and agave nectar in a blender, and process until smooth, thick, and creamy. Pour the filling into the prepared crust. Refrigerate for 2–3 hours before serving.

Tropical Paradise Pie

Yield: 6–8 servings

Crust

2 cups	pecans, soaked 1 hour
½ cup	pitted dates, soaked 15 minutes

*P*lace the pecans in a food processor fitted with the S blade, and process into a fine meal. Gradually add the dates, and continue processing until the dough forms a ball. Press into a 9-inch glass pie plate.

Filling

½ cup	macadamia nuts, soaked 1 hour
2 cups	young coconut pulp
2	large ripe bananas
1 tablespoon	psyllium powder
1 teaspoon	fresh lemon juice
1 teaspoon	vanilla extract
1	large very ripe mango, cut into ¼-inch-thick slices
	Unsweetened shredded dried coconut

Combine the macadamia nuts and coconut pulp in a blender, and process until smooth, thick, and creamy. Add the bananas, psyllium powder, lemon juice, and vanilla extract, and process until smooth. Arrange the mango slices evenly over the bottom of the prepared crust. Pour the blended filling over the mango. Sprinkle the top with dried coconut. Refrigerate for 2–3 hours before serving.

Coconut Crème Pie

Yield: 6–8 servings

Crust

2 cups	hazelnuts, soaked 1 hour
2 cups	unsweetened shredded dried coconut
¼ cup	pitted dates
1 tablespoon	raw coconut oil

Place the hazelnuts in a food processor fitted with the S blade, and process into a fine meal. Gradually add the dried coconut, dates, and coconut oil, and process until well blended. Add a small amount of water, as needed, to facilitate blending and achieve the desired consistency. Press into a 9-inch glass pie plate.

Filling

3 cups	young coconut pulp
1 cup	macadamia nuts or cashews, soaked 1 hour
3 tablespoons	agave nectar
1 teaspoon	coconut extract

Combine the coconut pulp, macadamia nuts, agave nectar, and coconut extract in a blender, and process until smooth, thick, and creamy. Add a small amount of water to facilitate blending and achieve the desired consistency. Pour the filling into the prepared crust. Refrigerate for 2–3 hours before serving.

Raspberry Crème Pie with Mango Filling

Yield: 6–8 servings

Crust

2 cups	hazelnuts, soaked 1 hour
1/2 cup	pitted medjool dates

Place the hazelnuts in a food processor fitted with the S blade, and process into a fine meal. Gradually add the dates, and continue processing until the dough forms a ball. Press into a 9-inch glass pie plate.

Filling

2 cups	young coconut pulp
1 1/2 cups	fresh or frozen raspberries
1/4 cup	pitted dates, soaked 1 hour
1 tablespoon	psyllium powder
1 teaspoon	vanilla extract
1	large ripe mango, sliced

Combine the coconut pulp, raspberries, and dates in a blender, and process until smooth, thick, and creamy. Add the psyllium powder and vanilla extract, and mix well. Arrange the mango slices evenly on the bottom of the prepared crust. Pour the blended filling over the mango, and refrigerate for 2–3 hours before serving.

111

Blackberry Crème Pie
with Banana Filling

Crust

2 cups	almonds, soaked 12–48 hours and dehydrated 18–24 hours
2 cups	unsweetened shredded dried coconut
1 tablespoon	raw coconut oil

Place the almonds in a food processor fitted with the S blade, and process into a fine meal. Gradually add the dried coconut and coconut oil, and process until well blended. Add a small amount of water, as needed, to facilitate blending. Press into a 9-inch glass pie plate.

Filling

2 cups	young coconut pulp
1½ cups	fresh or frozen blackberries
¼ cup	pitted dates, soaked 1 hour
1 tablespoon	psyllium powder
1	ripe banana, sliced

Combine the coconut pulp, blackberries, and dates in a blender, and process until smooth, thick, and creamy. Add the psyllium powder, and mix well. Arrange the banana slices evenly on the bottom of the prepared crust. Pour the filling over the banana. Refrigerate for 2–3 hours before serving.

Decorations for the Top

1	kiwi, sliced
3	strawberries
	Mint leaves

Decorate the top with the kiwi slices, forming a spiral in the center of the pie. Arrange the strawberries and mint leaves in the center of the spiral.

Piña Colada Pie

See photo facing page 97.

See photo facing page 97.

Yield: 6–8 servings

Crust

2 cups	pecans, soaked 1 hour
2 cups	unsweetened shredded dried coconut

Place the pecans in a food processor fitted with the S blade, and process into a fine meal. Gradually add the dried coconut, and process until well blended. Press into a 9-inch glass pie plate.

Filling

2 cups	chopped fresh or frozen pineapple
1 cup	macadamia nuts or cashews, soaked 1 hour
1½ cups	young coconut pulp
1 teaspoon	vanilla extract

Combine the pineapple and macadamia nuts in a blender, and process until smooth, thick, and creamy. Add the coconut pulp and vanilla extract, and process until smooth. Pour the filling into the prepared crust, and refrigerate for 2–3 hours before serving.

Decorations for the Top

1	kiwi, sliced
5	raspberries
	Mint leaves

Decorate the top with the kiwi slices, forming a spiral in the center of the pie. Arrange the raspberries and mint leaves in the center of the spiral.

Apple Pie

Crust

2 cups	almonds, soaked 12–48 hours
1/2 cup	pitted dates
2 tablespoons	raw almond butter
1/4 teaspoon	Celtic salt

Place the almonds in a food processor fitted with the S blade, and process into a fine meal. Gradually add the dates, almond butter, and salt, and continue processing until the dough forms a ball. Press into a 9-inch glass pie plate.

Filling

4	Fuji apples, peeled, cored, and cut into chunks
1/2 cup	pitted medjool dates, soaked 1 hour
1/2 cup	raisins, soaked 1 hour
2 tablespoons	psyllium powder
1/2 teaspoon	ground cinnamon
1/2 teaspoon	ground ginger
1/8 teaspoon	ground allspice
1/8 teaspoon	ground cloves
4	Fuji apples, peeled, cored, and thinly sliced

Place the apple chunks in a blender, and process until smooth. Add the dates, raisins, psyllium powder, cinnamon, ginger, allspice, and cloves, and process until well blended. Arrange the sliced apples evenly on the bottom of the prepared crust. Pour the blended filling over the sliced apples. Refrigerate for 2–3 hours before serving.

Apple Cranberry Pie

Crust

2 cups	pecans, soaked 1 hour
¼ cup	pitted medjool dates
¼ cup	raisins, soaked 1 hour

Place the pecans in a food processor fitted with the S blade, and process into a fine meal. Gradually add the dates and raisins, and continue processing until well blended. Press into a 9-inch glass pie plate.

Filling

4	Fuji apples, peeled, cored, and cut into chunks
1 cup	pitted medjool dates
2 teaspoons	psyllium powder
1 teaspoon	ground cinnamon
¼ teaspoon	ground nutmeg
1 cup	dried cranberries, soaked 1 hour
4	Fuji apples, peeled, cored, and thinly sliced

Place the apple chunks in a blender, and process until smooth. Add the dates, psyllium powder, cinnamon, and nutmeg, and process until well blended. Stir in the cranberries. Arrange the sliced apples evenly on the bottom of the prepared crust. Pour the blended filling over the sliced apples. Refrigerate for 2–3 hours before serving.

Key Lime Pie

Yield: 6–8 servings

Crust

2 cups	almonds, soaked 12–48 hours and dehydrated 18 hours
2 cups	unsweetened shredded dried coconut
1 tablespoon	raw coconut oil

*P*lace the almonds in a food processor fitted with the S blade, and process into a fine meal. Gradually add the dried coconut and coconut oil, and process until well blended. Press into a 9-inch glass pie plate.

Filling

3 cups	young coconut pulp
1/2 cup	macadamia nuts or cashews, soaked 1 hour
1/3 cup	pitted dates, soaked 15 minutes
1/4 cup	young coconut water
1/2	large ripe avocado
4 tablespoons	fresh lemon juice
4 tablespoons	fresh lime juice
1 tablespoon	agave nectar
1 tablespoon	psyllium powder
2 teaspoons	vanilla extract

Combine the coconut pulp, macadamia nuts, dates, and coconut water in a blender, and process until smooth, thick, and creamy. Add the avocado, lemon juice, lime juice, agave nectar, psyllium powder, and vanilla extract, and process until smooth. Pour the filling into the prepared crust, and refrigerate for 2–3 hours before serving.

Decoration for the Top

　　　　1　　lime, sliced

Decorate the top of the pie with the lime slices.

Lemon Fantasy Pie

Crust

2 cups	almonds, soaked 12–48 hours and dehydrated 18 hours
2 cups	unsweetened shredded dried coconut
1 tablespoon	raw coconut oil

Place the almonds in a food processor fitted with the S blade, and process into a fine meal. Gradually add the dried coconut and coconut oil, and process until well blended. Press into a 9-inch glass pie plate.

Filling

3 cups	young coconut pulp
1/2 cup	macadamia nuts or cashews, soaked 1 hour
1/2 cup	pitted dates, soaked 15 minutes
4 tablespoons	fresh lemon juice
2 tablespoons	grated lemon zest
1 tablespoon	psyllium powder

Combine the coconut pulp, macadamia nuts, and dates in a blender, and process until smooth, thick, and creamy. Add the lemon juice, lemon zest, and psyllium powder, and process until smooth. Pour the filling into the prepared crust, and refrigerate for 2–3 hours before serving.

Dreamy Carob Pie

Yield: 6–8 servings

Crust

2 cups	hazelnuts, soaked 1 hour
1 cup	pitted dates

Place the hazelnuts in a food processor fitted with the S blade, and process into a fine meal. Gradually add the dates, and continue processing until the dough forms a ball. Press into a 9-inch glass pie plate.

Filling

3 cups	young coconut pulp
1/2 cup	young coconut water
1/2 cup	macadamia nuts or cashews, soaked 1 hour
1/2 cup	pitted medjool dates
1/2	ripe avocado
4 tablespoons	raw carob powder
1 tablespoon	psyllium powder
2 tablespoons	vanilla extract

Combine the coconut pulp, coconut water, and macadamia nuts in a blender, and process until smooth, thick, and creamy. Add the dates, avocado, carob powder, psyllium powder, and vanilla extract, and process until smooth. Pour the filling into the prepared crust, and refrigerate for 2–3 hours before serving.

Mud Pie

Yield: 6–8 servings

Crust

2¹/₂ cups	pecans, soaked 1 hour
¹/₂ cup	pitted medjool dates
¹/₂ cup	dried Black Mission figs, soaked 30 minutes
3 tablespoons	raw cacao nibs, ground superfine

Place the pecans in a food processor fitted with the S blade, and process into a fine meal. Gradually add the dates, figs, and cacao nibs, and continue processing until the dough forms a ball. Press into a 9-inch glass pie plate.

Filling

1¹/₂ cups	almonds, soaked 12–48 hours and blanched (see page 10)
1 cup	young coconut water or water
3	ripe bananas
3 tablespoons	raw cacao nibs, ground superfine
2 tablespoons	agave nectar
1 teaspoon	vanilla extract

Combine all the ingredients in a blender, and process until smooth and creamy. Pour the filling into the prepared crust. Place the pie in the freezer for 3–4 hours before serving, or until firm. Store leftover pie in the freezer.

About the Author

Rose Lee Calabro is the author of *Living in the Raw* and *Living in the Raw Gourmet*. She discovered raw living food over eleven years ago in a class given by Pam Masters (*Living in the Raw* is dedicated to Pam). In a very short time she began to have more energy and lost a great deal of weight, and her body began to heal very quickly. Prior to going raw, Rose Lee had experienced a host of health issues, including cancer, gout, chronic fatigue, high cholesterol, high blood pressure, joint pain, depression, hypoglycemia, chronic sinusitis, and gallstones. Healing takes place on a physical, emotional, and spiritual level, and Rose Lee continues to improve her health and have new awakenings about herself. It has been an incredible journey!

Rose Lee has dedicated her life to teaching raw and living food and inspiring and motivating people to make positive changes in their lives.

Index

Index